Stella Maidment and Lorena Roberts

Happy House
New Edition

Class Book 1

OXFORD
UNIVERSITY PRESS

1 Welcome to Happy House!

4 | Unit 1 Lesson 1 | Listen and point. Listen and say. Listen, then sing: The hello song.

Mum Dad Polly Jack Daisy Otto Hello, I'm (Mum).

1. Listen to the story. Act out the story.

Unit 1 Lesson 2

Come in! What's your name? Goodbye. Spike Ruby

AB p3

1 Listen and say.  Then ask your friends.

Unit 1 Lesson 3

What's your name? I'm (Rodney).

1 🎧 **Listen and say the chant: Who's this?**

8 Unit 1 Lesson 4

Who's this? Let's see. It's (Jack). It's me! AB p5

Order the pictures. 1 Then listen and point.

CROSS-CURRICULAR LINKS

Unit 1 Lesson 5

Sequencing:
Hello. Come in! It's Otto! Goodbye.

1 🎧 Listen to the story. 🎭 Act out the story.

Unit 1 Lesson 6

Good morning.   Sit down!   What's the matter?

1 (11-12) Sing: The Happy House song.

✂ **Take-home English:** Make a house.

Unit 1 Lesson 7

It's a house. Here's a (window).
door roof floor

AB p59

11

2 Pens and pencils

12 Unit 2 Lesson 1 1 (13) Listen and point. Listen and say. 1 (14–16) Listen, then sing: What's in my bag?

a bag   a book   a ruler   a pencil   a pen   a pencil-case
What's in my bag?   There's a (book).

1 🎧 Listen to the story. 🎭 Act out the story.

14 Unit 2 Lesson 2

What's this? It's a (pencil). I don't know. Yes. No.

AB p11

1. Listen and point. Then look and say. Now play the game.

Unit 2 Lesson 3

What's this? It's a (book).

1 (20-22) Listen, then sing: Ten little fingers.

16 Unit 2 Lesson 4   one two three four five six seven eight nine ten   AB p13

1 (23) Listen and point. Then look and say.

1

2

3

Unit 2 Lesson 5

Counting (one more):
(One) and one more is (two).

AB p14 **17**

1. **Listen to the story.** **Act out the story.**

Unit 2 Lesson 6

Look! How many (pencils)?

1 (25–26) Sing: The number conga.

 **Take-home English:** Make and play number pairs.

Unit 2 Lesson 7

Come on everybody! Dance with me.
Now it's ten. Dance again.

3 Come and play!

20 Unit 3 Lesson 1   1 ²⁷ Listen and point. Listen and say.   1 ²⁸⁻³⁰ Listen, then sing: The toy song.

a doll   a train   a car   a plane   a guitar   a drum
Look, Daisy, here's a (doll)!

1 🔊 Listen to the story. 🎭 Act out the story.

Unit 3 Lesson 2

One, two, three, four dolls / cakes.
Come on!   Quick!   Naughty cat.

1 🔊32 Listen and point.  Then play the game.

Unit 3 Lesson 3 (Four) (planes). Picture (one).

1 (33–35) Listen, then sing: The colour song.

24 Unit 3 Lesson 4

red green yellow orange pink blue
(Red) in my rainbow. Can you see? Paint with me!

AB p21

1 🎧37 Listen and point. Listen and say.

1 🎧38 Listen.   Then play the game.

Unit 3 Lesson 5

Shapes:
Eight (squares), one (circle), one (triangle).

CROSS-CURRICULAR LINKS

AB p22

25

1 🎧 Listen to the story. 🎭 Act out the story.

Unit 3 Lesson 6

Here's a (red) pen.
(Please) be quiet! Stop it!

1 (40–41) Sing: Noisy toys.

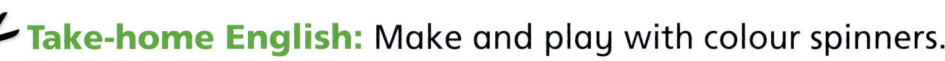

Take-home English: Make and play with colour spinners.

Unit 3 Lesson 7

Let's have fun with noisy toys!
Beat the drum!   Play the guitar!   Fly the plane!   Drive the car!

AB p63   **27**

Me and my family

1. 🔊 ⁴² Listen. Who's this?

1 🎧 Listen. Who's five?

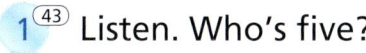

Talk about your family.

Culture

This is my family.
mum dad sister brother

29

4 Dressing up

30 Unit 4 Lesson 1   1 (44) Listen and point. Listen and say.   1 (45–46) Listen, then say the chant: Where's my T-shirt?

a T-shirt   a skirt   a shoe   a hat   a jumper   a sock
Where's my (T-shirt)?

1 🎧47 Listen to the story. 🎭 Act out the story.

32 Unit 4 Lesson 2

One red sock.   Two red socks.
Be careful!   Here you are.   Thank you.

AB p27

1. Listen and point.  Then play the game.

Unit 4 Lesson 3

(One) (red) (hat).

1 ⁽⁵⁰⁻⁵²⁾ Listen, then sing: My favourite T-shirt.

34 Unit 4 Lesson 4

My favourite (T-shirt).
washing machine   jeans   clean

AB p29

1 🔊 **Listen and point. Then look and say.**

1

2

3

4

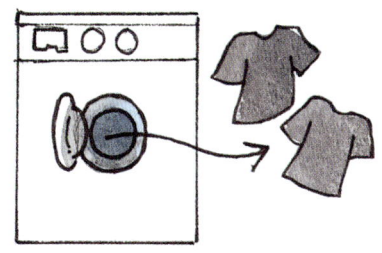

Unit 4 Lesson 5

Colour mixing:
One black T-shirt and one white T-shirt. Two grey T-shirts!

AB p30   **35**

1 🎭 Listen to the story. 🎭 Act out the story.

36 Unit 4 Lesson 6

This is my favourite song.
What's your favourite song? Listen!

AB p31

1 (55-56) **Sing:** And don't forget your hat!

✂ **Take-home English:** Make mix-and-match people.

Unit 4 Lesson 7

Put on your (T-shirt)! Take off your (socks and shoes)! Don't forget your hat! trousers

AB p65

37

5 Happy birthday!

38 Unit 5 Lesson 1   2① Listen and point. Listen and say.   2②⁻④ Listen, then sing: It's my birthday.

a present   a card   a candle   a cake   a badge   a balloon
I've got (a present).   It's my birthday today.

2 Listen to the story. Act out the story.

40 Unit 5 Lesson 2

Is it a bike / car?   Come and see!
For you.   For me?   Open it!

AB p35

2 🔊 Listen. Then play the game.

Unit 5 Lesson 3   Is it a (balloon)?   Is it a (blue balloon)?   Number 3.   AB p36   41

2 **Listen, then say the chant: How old are you?**

1

2

3

42 Unit 5 Lesson 4

How old are you? I'm seven.
Are you (one)? How many candles on your cake?

AB p37

2 **Listen and point. Then say.**

1

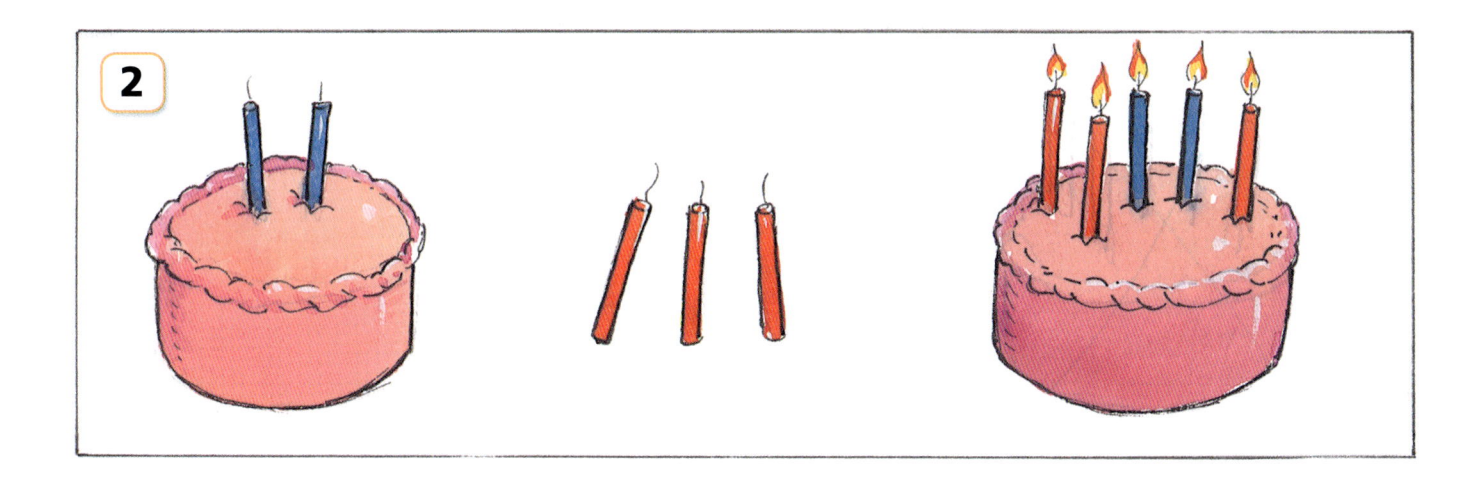

2

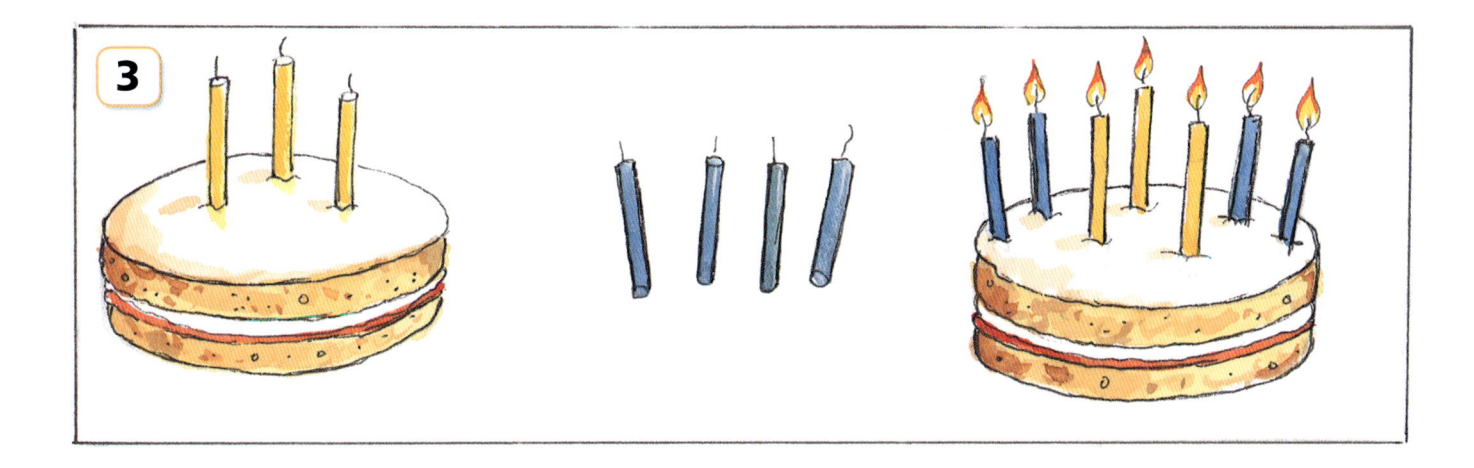

3

Unit 5 Lesson 5

Simple addition:
One candle … and two candles … three candles!

CROSS-CURRICULAR LINKS

2 (12–13) Listen to the story. 🎭 Act out the story. Then sing: Happy birthday!

Unit 5 Lesson 6

What's that? Is it the radio / television?
Open the card!

AB p39

2. **Sing:** The party freeze.

✂ **Take-home English:** Make a birthday game.

Unit 5 Lesson 7

Jump! Dance! Shake! Clap!
Stamp your feet! Freeze!

AB p67

45

Party time!

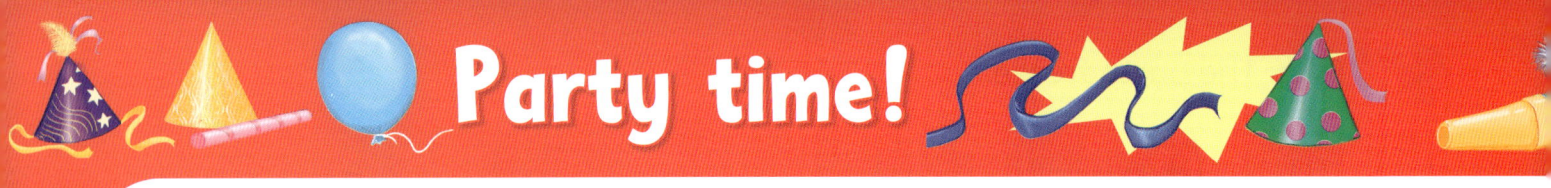

2 🔊18 Listen. What's Harry's present?

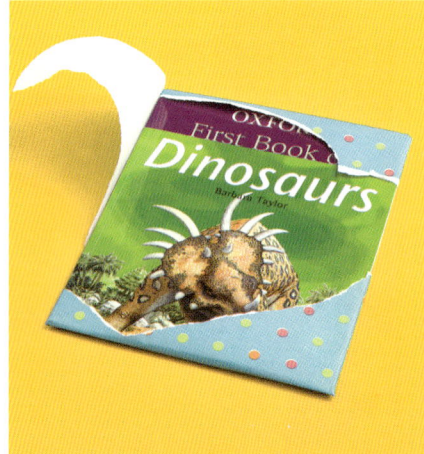

46 Culture

2 🔊 Listen. What's Anna's favourite food?

Play the party game.

Culture

grapes   sandwiches   ice cream
a party bag   sweets   stickers   a green dinosaur

47

6 Bathtime!

48 | Unit 6 Lesson 1 | 2⁽²⁰⁾ Listen and point. Listen and say. | 2⁽²¹⁻²³⁾ Listen, then sing: The bathtime song.

a hairbrush   a toothbrush   soap   shampoo   a towel   a duck
Here's your (hairbrush).

49

2. Listen to the story. Act out the story.

50 Unit 6 Lesson 2

Can you see me? Where are you? Here I am! Are you OK?
Can you climb up? No, I can't. You're welcome.

AB p43

2 Listen and point. Then ask your friend. Now ask about your classroom.

Unit 6 Lesson 3

Can you see a (door)?

51

2 (27-29) Listen, then sing: I wash my hands.

52 Unit 6 Lesson 4

*Every day I wash my hands / face.
I brush my teeth / hair.   clean and tidy*

AB p45

2 🔊 Listen and point. Then look and say.

CROSS-CURRICULAR LINKS

Unit 6 Lesson 5

Science:
It's cold / warm / hot.

AB p46

53

2 Listen to the story. Act out the story.

54 Unit 6 Lesson 6

Wash your (face)! Dry your (hands)!
Good girl. That's better.

AB p47

2 (33–34) Sing: I can do anything.

Take-home English: Ask your family!

Unit 6 Lesson 7

Can you click your fingers / touch your toes / wink your eye / see your nose?   Yes, I can.

55

7 Animal friends

Unit 7 Lesson 1   2 (36) Listen and point. Listen and say.   2 (37–39) Listen, then sing: Animal friends.

a dog a cat a bird a snake a mouse a tiger
Say goodnight. There's a (dog) in the house.

AB p50

57

2 🎧 Listen to the story. 🎭 Act out the story.

58 Unit 7 Lesson 2

Wake up!   Do you like dogs?   Hide in the cupboard!

AB p51

2 Listen and point. Then ask your friend.

1
2
3
4
5
6

Unit 7 Lesson 3

Do you like (birds)?   Yes, I do.   No, I don't.
a shark   a rabbit   a crocodile

AB p52

59

2 (42–43) Listen, then say the chant: Where's Otto?

60 Unit 7 Lesson 4

Where's Otto? On the chair. In the bed / box.

AB p53

2 ⁽⁴⁵⁻⁴⁶⁾ Listen and point. Then listen and answer.

CROSS-CURRICULAR LINKS

Unit 7 Lesson 5

Science:
Where do (tigers) live? On land. In water.

AB p54

61

2 🎧(47) Listen to the story. 🎭 Act out the story.

62 Unit 7 Lesson 6

What's the matter?   Rabbit's on the floor.
It's OK.   Don't cry!   Daddy's here.

AB p55

2 (49-50) Sing: Are you happy?

Take-home English: Make and play a game.

Unit 7 Lesson 7

Clap your hands! Stamp your feet! Shout 'Hooray'!

AB p71

63

Pets

2 (51) Listen and point. Then say.

64 | Culture

sit run jump

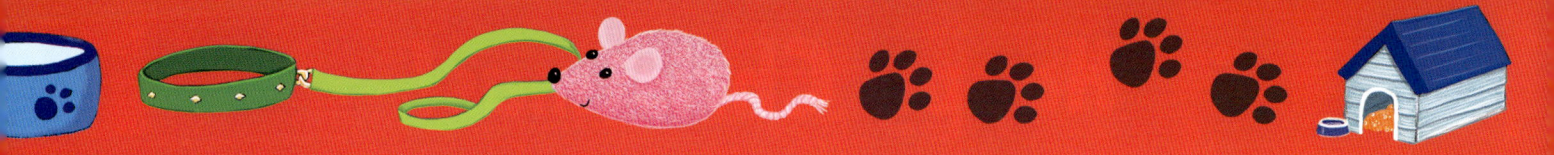

2 ⁵² Listen and answer. Ask your friends.

Make a chart.

Culture

a goldfish   a hamster

65

Happy Christmas!

2 🔊 Listen and point. Then count.

Festivals

a Christmas tree   a bell   a star   a fairy

2 ⁽⁵⁴⁾ Listen. What's in Anna's Christmas stocking?

2 ⁽⁵⁵⁻⁵⁶⁾ Sing: We wish you a merry Christmas!

Make a Christmas tree.

Festivals

a Christmas stocking

67

Happy Easter!

2. Listen. What day is it today?

68 Festivals

Easter Day   an Easter egg
chocolate   a rabbit   a chicken

2 (58) Listen. How many eggs in Anna's basket?

2 (59–60) Sing: The Easter egg song.

Look for Easter eggs.

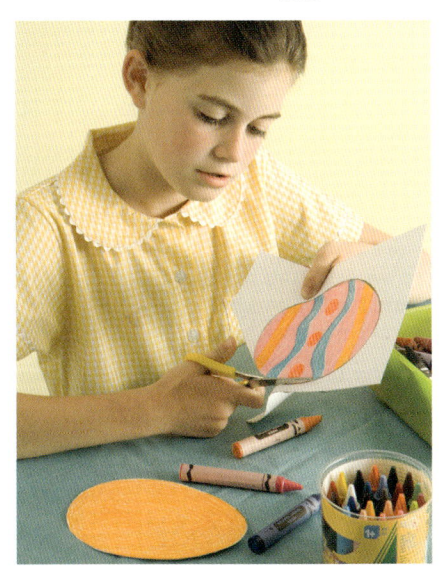

Festivals

a basket   flowers

69

Happy House songs

Unit 1

The hello song *page 4*
Hello, I'm Mum.
Hello, I'm Dad.
Hello, I'm Polly.
Hello, I'm Jack.

Happy House family
Happy House family
Miaow! I'm Otto.
Miaow! Miaow! Miaow!

Chant: Who's this? *page 8*
Who's this?
Let's see.
It's Jack!
It's me!

Who's this?
Let's see.
It's Polly!
It's me!

Who's this?
Let's see.
It's Dad!
It's me!

The Happy House song *page 11*
It's a house,
It's a happy house,
It's a happy house,
Can you see?

Here's a window,
Here's a door,
Here's a roof,
And here's a floor!

It's a house,
It's a happy house,
It's a happy house,
For you and me!

Unit 2

What's in my bag? *page 12*
What's in my bag?
There's a book. A book!
What's in my bag?
There's a ruler. A ruler!

What's in my bag?
There's a pencil. A pencil!
What's in my bag?
There's a pen. A pen!

There's a book, there's a ruler,
There's a pencil, there's a pen.
What's in my bag?
There's a pencil-case!

Ten little fingers *page 16*
One, two, three,
Three little fingers.
Four, five, six,
Six little fingers.
Seven, eight, nine,
Nine little fingers,
Ten little fingers
Clap! Clap! Clap!

One, two, three,
Three little fingers.
Four, five, six,
Six little fingers.
Seven, eight, nine,
Nine little fingers,
Ten little fingers
Clap! Clap! Clap!

The number conga *page 19*
Come on everybody
Do the number conga!
One, two, three,
Dance with me!

Come on everybody
Do the number conga!
Four, five, six,
Dance like this!

Come on everybody
Do the number conga!
Seven, eight, nine,
Dance in line!

Come on everybody
Do the number conga!
Now it's ten,
Dance again!

Unit 3

The toy song *page 20*
Look, Daisy, here's a doll.
Daisy, here's a train.
Look, Daisy, here's a car.
Daisy, here's a plane.

Look, Daisy, here's a guitar.
Daisy, here's a drum.
Rum pum pum pum - pum pum pum
Rum ta ta pum, pum, pum!

Look, Daisy, here's a doll.
Daisy, here's a train.
Look, Daisy, here's a car.
Daisy, here's a plane.

Look, Daisy, here's a guitar.
Daisy, here's a drum.
Rum pum pum pum - pum pum pum
Rum ta ta pum, pum, pum!

The colour song *page 24*
Red in my rainbow,
Green in my rainbow,
Yellow in my rainbow,
Can you see?

Orange in my rainbow,
Pink in my rainbow,
Blue in my rainbow,
Paint with me!

Noisy toys *page 27*
Noisy toys! Noisy toys!
Let's have fun with noisy toys!

Beat the drum!
Rum pum pum!
Beat the drum!
Rum pum pum!

Noisy toys! Noisy toys!
Let's have fun with noisy toys!

Play the guitar!
Strum strum strum!
Play the guitar!
Strum strum strum!

Noisy toys! Noisy toys!
Let's have fun with noisy toys!

Fly the plane!
Neee-ow!
Fly the plane!
Neee-ow!

Noisy toys! Noisy toys!
Let's have fun with noisy toys!

Drive the car!
Brrm Brrm Brrm!
Drive the car!
Brrm Brrm Brrm!

Noisy toys! Noisy toys!
Let's have fun with noisy toys!

Unit 4

Chant: Where's my T-shirt? *page 30*
Polly! Jack!
Where's my T-shirt?
Polly! Jack!
Where's my skirt?
Where's my shoe?
And where's my hat?
Where's my jumper?
Where's my sock?

Dressing up!
Having fun!
Now I'm Dad!
Now I'm Mum!

My favourite T-shirt page 34
My favourite jumper in the washing machine,
The washing machine, the washing machine,
My favourite jumper in the washing machine,
Now my jumper is clean!
Oh yes!
Now my jumper is clean!

My favourite T-shirt in the washing machine,
The washing machine, the washing machine,
My favourite T-shirt in the washing machine,
Now my T-shirt is green!
Oh no!
Now my T-shirt is green!

And don't forget your hat! page 37
Put on your T-shirt,
Your T-shirt,
Your T-shirt.
Put on your T-shirt!
And don't forget your hat!

Put on your trousers, . . .

Put on your socks and shoes, . . .

Take off your socks and shoes!
Socks and shoes,
Socks and shoes.
Take off your socks and shoes!
And don't forget your hat!

Take off your trousers, . . .

Take off your T-shirt, . . .

Unit 5

It's my birthday page 38
I've got a present
It's my birthday.
I've got a card
It's my birthday.
I've got a candle
It's my birthday,
It's my birthday today!

I've got a cake
It's my birthday.
I've got a badge
It's my birthday.
I've got a balloon
It's my birthday. POP!
It's my birthday today!

Chant: How old are you? page 42
How old are you? How old are you?
Are you one? Or are you two?
Are you six? Or are you eight?
How many candles on your cake?
How old are you?

I'm seven!

How old are you? How old are you?
Are you one? Or are you two?
Are you six? Or are you eight?
How many candles on your cake?
How old are you?

I'm seven!

Happy birthday! page 44
Happy birthday to you,
Happy birthday to you,
Happy birthday, dear Polly,
Happy birthday to you.

Happy birthday to you,
Happy birthday to you,
Happy birthday, dear Jack,
Happy birthday to you.

The party freeze page 45
Jump, jump, jump to the party music!
Dance, dance, dance to the party beat!
Shake, shake, shake to the party music!
Clap, clap, clap! And stamp your feet!
But when the music stops,
When the music stops,
When the music stops . . .
FREEZE!

Unit 6

The bathtime song page 48
Here's your hairbrush, hairbrush, hairbrush,
Bathtime fun. Splish, splosh.

Here's your toothbrush, toothbrush, toothbrush,
Bathtime fun. Splish, splosh.

Here's your soap and your shampoo,
Bathtime fun. Splish, splosh.

Here's your towel and here's your duck,
Bathtime fun. Quack! quack! quack!

I wash my hands page 52
Every day I wash my hands,
Wash my hands, wash my hands,
Every day I wash my hands
Then I'm clean and tidy!

Every day I wash my face,
Wash my face, wash my face,
Every day I wash my face
Then I'm clean and tidy!

Every day I brush my teeth,
Brush my teeth, brush my teeth,
Every day I brush my teeth
Then I'm clean and tidy!

Every day I brush my hair,
Brush my hair, brush my hair,
Every day I brush my hair
Then I'm clean and tidy!

I can do anything page 55
I can do anything, anything, anything!
I can do anything. What about you?

Can you click your fingers?
Yes, I can.
Can you touch your toes?
Yes, I can.

Can you wink your eye?
Yes, I can.
Can you see your nose?
Yes, I can.

I can do anything, anything, anything!
I can do anything, just like you!

Unit 7

Animal friends page 56
There's a dog in the house
Woof! Woof! Woof!
There's a cat in the house
Miaow!
There's a bird in the house
Tweet! Tweet! Tweet!
There's a snake in the house
OH WOW!

Animal friends, animal friends,
Say 'Goodnight' to my animal friends.

There's a dog in the house
Woof! Woof! Woof!
There's a cat in the house
Miaow!
There's a mouse in the house
Eek! Eek! Eek!
There's a tiger in the house
OH WOW!

Animal friends, animal friends,
Say 'Goodnight' to my animal friends.

Chant: Where's Otto? *page 60*
Where's Otto?
On the dog.
Where's the dog?
On the snake.
Where's the snake?
On the tiger.
Where's the tiger?
In the box.
Where's the box?
In the cupboard.
Where's Otto?
In the cupboard.
In the cupboard?
YES!

Are you happy? *page 63*
Are you happy? Are you happy?
Clap your hands!
Are you happy? Are you happy?
Clap your hands!
I'm a happy little mouse,
In a happy little house,
And if you're happy too
Clap your hands!

Are you happy? Are you happy?
Stamp your feet!
Are you happy? Are you happy?
Stamp your feet!
I'm a happy little mouse,
In a happy little house,
And if you're happy too
Stamp your feet!

Are you happy? Are you happy?
Shout 'Hooray'!
Are you happy? Are you happy?
Shout 'Hooray'!
I'm a happy little mouse,
In a happy little house,
And if you're happy too
Shout 'Hooray'!

Festivals

We wish you a merry Christmas *page 67*
We wish you a merry Christmas,
We wish you a merry Christmas,
We wish you a merry Christmas,
And a happy new year!

We wish you a merry Christmas,
We wish you a merry Christmas,
We wish you a merry Christmas,
And a happy new year!

The Easter egg song *page 69*
Let's all look for Easter eggs
Easter eggs, Easter eggs!
Let's all look for Easter eggs,
It's Easter Day today!

Let's all look for Easter eggs
Easter eggs, Easter eggs!
Let's all look for Easter eggs,
It's Easter Day today!